I'm Engaged! Now What?

By EJ Divitt

Congratulations! You are engaged! You are probably incredibly excited. I bet you keep sneaking looks at that sparkling ring on your finger and waving it around to catch the light. Maybe you had a manicure or did your nails in anticipation of everyone looking at your hand. You are thrilled and ecstatic and maybe a little scared or overwhelmed.

Suddenly you realize you have a wedding to plan. Where do you start? What do you need to do? There are probably a thousand things going through your head but let's see if we can put them in some kind of order.

First you need to tell the important people in your life. Make sure they hear it from one of you and not from a third party. Do not let your parents read it on Facebook or Twitter before they hear it from you. Pick up the phone and call them. After you have told the most important people in your life, feel free to send out a mass email. Go ahead and tweet it or change your status on

Facebook. Stand at the end of your driveway and yell, "I'm engaged!"

Second, you need to have a couple of big conversations with your fiance. What kind of wedding do you want? The first thing you need to nail down is what kind of ceremony you both want. Sit down and have a serious talk about what you want. You will also need to consider what your families want as well but don't let that be the whole focus of your planning. Be prepared to compromise! You are not buying anything at this point. You are just brainstorming. This can change as new options present themselves but you need a place to start.

Here are some things to think about in terms of what kind of wedding you want to have.

Indoors or outdoors? Are you thinking country club or beach?   Park or temple?

Religious or secular? You can decide to get married in a church or a park or the town hall.

Do you want to keep it small or invite everyone you know? (or something in between)

Fancy or casual?

Is there going to be a theme such as everyone wears black and silver or the decorations are all Hawaiian themed?

Destination wedding or local one? You could travel to Las Vegas or get married at the local park or on a cruise ship.

Do you want to dress up in a fancy gown or tux? Would you prefer a suit or cocktail dress? Maybe you want to wear a costume or get married in jeans. It is up to the two of you. Feel free to brainstorm and come out with any number of outlandish ideas.

This is not the time to decide that you want 30 swans swimming around a castle. This is just to decide on the basics. Indoor/outdoor etc

Of course if you decide to just elope, you can skip the most of this and go straight to the part where you explain it to your families.

Once you have an idea of the type of wedding you want, then you need to have the dreaded money talk. This means having a serious conversation about what you can afford to spend and what you are willing to spend. This will be your wedding budget and will dictate a lot of your future choices.

Remember you have a marriage to pay for after the wedding is over. Maybe you have $25,000 in the bank. Are you sure you want to spend that on the wedding? Maybe you would prefer to spend $10,000 and have the savings towards a house or a child?

I would recommend that you think twice before taking out a loan for the wedding. I know it is tempting to borrow the money so you can have the big elaborate day of your dreams. Before you do, decide if you want to be paying for that day for years to come. It could delay you being able to pay off student loans or get a house. Now would be the time to set up a savings plan if you plan to save up for your wedding. Set the plan and stick to it.

Do not assume that the bride's parents will pay for the wedding. While it was tradition, it was tradition based on the fact that the young couple would have no home or resources of their own to draw on. People are waiting longer these days to get married. They often have homes or apartments of their own before getting married. You can sit your parents down and politely ask them if they would be able to help you with paying for the wedding. Whatever their answer, thank them graciously. If you are disappointed with their answer, keep it to yourself until you are away from them. Do not complain to other family members that your parents are not helping you out.

Once you have a budget amount in mind, you can figure out what venue you can afford and how many people you can invite. Generally the more people you invite, the more the wedding will cost. You can lower this some if you chose a venue that is less expensive per plate or if you opt to go for a cocktail reception instead of a full meal.

You should decide what items you do not want to compromise on in terms of spending. Some things will be more important to you than others. For me it was the dress, the tux and the photographer. For you it may mean spending more for the country club for the reception or getting your favorite band.

It is customary to tip individuals who work at your wedding as long as they are not the owners of their own business. For instance, if you hire a large firm who sends out a DJ, you would tip the DJ. If he is a one man show, then it is not necessary to tip. People you would tip might include the hairdresser or the photographer.

Allow plenty of room in your budget for incidentals. They tend to add up. At the end of the book, you will find a list of the categories in the budget for my own wedding. I did not include prices as the prices of things will vary wildly around the country or world or even from year to year. These are just intended to give you categories to plan around.

Set up a wedding bank account. It could be savings or checking. This account should only ever hold money designated for the wedding costs. If your plan is to save a certain amount of money every week or month, you should set up to have it automatically transferred to this account.

You might want to insure your engagement ring. If your engagement ring is expensive, talk to your insurance agent about adding it to your home insurance policy in case something happens to it.

You need to pick a date for the wedding. It is probably the number one question people will ask you. (It may be the second after, "How did he ask you?") The choice of date will often be driven more by what kind of wedding you want then the date itself.

Exceptions include if you want to get married on the anniversary of the day you met or on a significant day such as December 13, 2014 (12/13/14). A lot of couples got married on April 5, 2006 (4/5/6) and July 7, 2007 (7/7/7).

Generally though, the wedding date will be at least partially influenced by where you are getting married. You need to consider the weather. You do not generally have an outdoor ceremony in Maine in January or in the desert in August. If you have a particular place you have decided to get married like a famous castle or the country club, your choice may be limited by what dates are available at that location.

You may need to be a little flexible about the date at this point. If you pick for example, July 19, 2014 and then find that there is a convention in town that day, you may want to change it. If you are planning to pick a three day weekend or a holiday, this may affect how many people attend. People often make plans for holidays or long weekends many months in advance.

Everything at this point is preliminary. You are just trying to get a framework so you can start to plan. Think of it like outlining an essay. You write the basics and then change it as you need to as it develops. You will need to choose a time of day at some point as well i.e. a morning ceremony, afternoon or evening.

Spend a lot of time looking at bridal magazines, searching bridal sites and staring at wedding dresses. You know you want to do it. Check out venues, hair styles, bridesmaids dresses, crafts for favors. Consider it research.

Set up a wedding board on www.pinterest.com or a similar site **or make a binder for the wedding** that you can put all of the paperwork and ideas in. You need a way to keep track of ideas and what decisions have been made and are yet to be made. When you browse online for ideas for dresses, venues, favors, bridesmaids dresses, you can "pin" them to www.pinterest.com and come back and see them later. Visit sites like www.theknot.com to get ideas. Have some fun but keep track of the things you like; that is why a site like www.pinterest.com is useful. You can make your board secret if you are embarrassed or just want to make it all a surprise. You should decide if you want to have a wedding website. At this time, you can get a free one from www.theknot.com. You should list all the information about your wedding on your wedding website such as where, when, who and how to get to the venues.

If you know anyone who has gotten married in the last few years, start picking their brains. They can be an excellent source of information on things to try or avoid. They may have the perfect DJ for you or let you know the caterer to avoid. Most people like to share their wedding stories and reminisce about the traps and surprises.

You will need to work on a preliminary guest list. Get your guest list, your fiance's and both sets of parents. Check for any duplicates. This will give you a jumping off point for your venue. If you plan to have 200 guests, you should not book the room that only holds 120.

Once you have decided on the date, you should decide if you want attendants. What kind of wedding you are having has a lot to do with how many you will need or want. If you plan a small ceremony, you may only want one maid of honor and one best man. If you are planning a big wedding, you may want several of each. What about flower girls or ring bearers? It is important to have a sense of the size of the wedding as being an attendant comes with a price tag. They need to buy or rent outfits. They probably need to do some traveling. Showers and bachelor parties need to be planned. If someone declines to be an attendant because of the cost, be understanding. It is expensive to be involved in a wedding and circumstances do not always allow. Be clear up front if you plan to have a large wedding or elaborate attendant outfits so they can make an informed decision. Every attendant gets a thank you gift at the rehearsal dinner.

Decide if you want a wedding planner or event coordinator. You may hire them separately or you may get one with your venue. If you would rather go it alone, then plan time to do that. You will probably find it simpler to hire a wedding planner or use a venue with an event coordinator. You will probably find it cheaper to do it yourself.

You will need to pick a venue. You have already decided what type of wedding you want to have. This helps narrow down where you want to actually have the wedding. Do you want to get married in the same place as the reception? Do you want the big church wedding and then to go to a reception hall from there? If so, pick a reception place fairly close to the ceremony. People will need to travel easily to the reception. You may need to pick a separate venue to have the rehearsal dinner. This would be smaller and include just immediate family, attendants and attendants dates/spouses. You will need to decide between a formal sit down dinner, buffet or cocktail reception with appetizers. If you are getting married in a church, you may need to attend premarital classes. Look into this and plan for it.

Have a discussion with your fiance on who is handling which parts of this. Some people will naturally be more involved than others. Feel free to designate areas such as he will handle the music and the honeymoon. Do what works best for you as a couple.

If you are getting married outside

or at home, you may need to rent chairs, tables, outside toilets or tents. Do not forget to factor this into your budget. If you are going with an all inclusive venue, they can probably arrange this for you. If you are getting married at someone's house, consider allowing time or money for landscaping before the big day. Photos are forever. You should plan to shop for essentials such as plates, cups, napkins, silverware, table cloths, drinks, salt and pepper shakers etc if you are going this route.

You will need invitations and possibly save the date cards. You can order them from a traditional stationary store. You can make them yourself by downloading templates or by purchasing invitation kits at craft stores. You can also use an online service where you pick them online and they mail you the final product. Make sure you allow time for the invitations to reach you, be assembled and mailed and still give people time to RSVP at least four weeks before the wedding. Do not order the invitations until you are certain of the date, time and venues. Set up a way of keeping track of RSVPs. It could be your wedding website or a spreadsheet on your computer or a list on the fridge. Just don't lose it. Before sending out the invitations or save the date cards, make sure you have everyone's names and addresses spelt correctly. This includes the names of their significant others. If your wedding has a theme or color scheme, keep to the theme for your save the date cards and invitations.

You will need to pick the caterer. If you choose a venue with food packages or its own caterer then you can pick from the list they give you. If you want to pick your own caterer, then you should start research things in the area and be prepared to go do taste tests. Are you serving liquor? You will need to decide between an open bar, limited open bar (basic liquor selections only) or cash bar.

You will need to decide where you are getting your cake. You can hire a professional. You can have a talented friend make it. You can often get a cake included with an all inclusive venue. How ever you do it, make sure you plan to have a taste test before finalizing your selections. If you are going with a professional, you can often purchase a small decorative cake for the photos and cake cutting but buy a simple sheet cake to be cut up and passed out. This lets you have the nice cake for show and photos without the cost of buying a big enough fancy cake to feed everyone. It can also let you have multiple flavors.

You will need to decide on a photographer. This could be a professional or your cousin who is good with a camera. It could be a lot of disposable cameras spread out around the tables. If you go the professional route, make sure you review their work to see if you like their style. They probably have a website with a list of prices and samples of photos.

You will need someone to perform the ceremony. If you choose a church or town hall, this will probably be included. You can hire a justice of the peace to come out to you or you can go to them.

You will need to plan transportation to the ceremony, from the ceremony to the reception and then back to your hotel or home or honeymoon. Look into town cars or limousines, check out antique cars or just plan to have someone leave your own car at the church for you.

You will need to decide on flowers. Pick a florist or get a bunch of potted plants. Would you rather have a long cascading bouquet or just hold a few daisies? Do you want boutonnieres for the groomsmen and fathers or corsages for the mothers? Do you want real flowers or artificial ones? Do you want arrangements on the tables?

You will need to pick your outfit and your accessories, your hair and makeup. Do you want manicures and pedicures? Make sure you do trial runs on hair and makeup with whomever you choose so that you know exactly what you want and how it will look on the big day. Before committing to a dress, go to lots of bridal stores and try on a little bit of everything. You never know what will look good on you until you have tried on a wedding dress. I would never have picked my dress myself off the rack but I ended up loving it. Do not be too set on what you will wear until you try it on and see how the style looks on you. Do not be disappointed if you have to try on dozens of dresses to find the right one. Leave time for fittings which can take several months.

Pick your wedding colors. These colors will determine decorations and most importantly, the color of the bridesmaids dresses.

Pick your attendants outfits. Would you like them in full length gowns or something short? Should they dress in jeans and a cowgirl hat or like someone from the forties? Traditional, modern or casual? Take the ladies and go shopping. Send the men to get suits or rent tuxedos. If it is a theme wedding, you will need to find costumes.

You will need to pick your music source. Do you want a band or a DJ? A string quartet or a mix of music played over your mp3 with speakers? You will need to narrow down a list of song choices before the wedding for such things as mother/son, father/daughter, first dance and last dance. If there are any songs you especially want played or not played, make a note of them. Take the time to go hear the band or DJ play or listen to samples of their work. You do not want to find out that day that you don't like their style.

Decide if you want to have wedding favors. If so, what kind? You can do a crazy assortment of things. Look online. Check out www.pinterest.com for ideas. You can make them yourself or order them online. If ordering, allow plenty of time. You can check out craft stores for ideas as well.

Decide where you want to register for gifts. You can choose one place or two or three. If you are having a smaller wedding, you will probably not register for as many things. Make sure you register for a variety of pricing levels. Some people will be looking for smaller gifts and some people will be looking for bigger ones. If you are hoping to encourage more people to give you cash, you can register for less things.

Decide if you want to write your own vows or have readings at the wedding. Look online for poems or bible readings or romantic quotes that you can use. Pick your readings and if you wish, someone to do the readings for you. You can also just have the officiant read them.

Look into hotel options for out of town guests. If you are getting married at a hotel ballroom, then just set it up with the hotel. If not, look into motels and hotels in the area. Make sure they are nice hotels in a nice area. Contact the hotel to see if you can set up a reduced rate for rooms for your wedding guests. Include this information in the invitations when they go out.

You will want to plan your honeymoon. This can be as elaborate or as simple as you like. Do you want to do a cruise to Europe? Take a drive into the mountains. Browse online and talk to your fiance. Decide somewhere that has special meaning for the two of you or some place neither of you have been.

If you do not already have passports, apply for them right away. Get it in your maiden name and book all travel in your maiden name. You will not have time to get your name legally changed before you leave for your honeymoon. Passports are required for most kinds of travel now a days.

You will need to buy wedding rings

for both of you. If you plan to wear your engagement ring with your wedding ring, be aware of how they look together. Also, the wedding ring goes on the finger first so it is closest to your heart.

You will need to get a license to get married. Check with the state you plan to marry in. Here in Massachusetts, you both have to go and apply for your license between 1 to 4 weeks in advance of the wedding date. One of you then has to go back in three days and pick up the license. The license is good for 30 days from the date it is issued. if you are having a destination wedding, find out what that locale's rules are. If you have been previously married, make sure you can provide documentation of your annulment or divorce.

You may need to buy extra things for your day such as a guest book or picture frame for people to sign. You may want special toasting glasses. You may need decorations or centerpieces.

You should plan to have somewhere for people to leave cards for you at the reception. If you are having it in a public venue, you should plan to have a closed container such as a decorative envelope box to reduce the chance of someone walking off with your wedding cards. It does sometimes happen in public places where the cards are laid out and easily seen. It is easy for a thief to grab a handful of cards and take off.

Get everything in writing. If you sign up a vendor such as the photographer, caterer etc be prepared to sign a contract and leave a deposit. Always pay by check or credit card and always get a receipt.

Make a list of what is due and when it is due. You will have a lot of vendors and details to coordinate. You can use a checklist (such as the one at the end of this ebook) or a spreadsheet.

Do not forget that all this is just a lead up to your marriage. The wedding is not the destination. It is just the flourish. Try not to get on each other's nerves or fight over the wedding. If you do, do not let it get out of hand. Apologize and move on.

Now that you know the basics, get out there and start planning your wedding! May you have a sunny day and a long happy life together.

Suggested Wedding Checklist

12 to 18 Months out

Set up your budget and start saving

Browse for ideas

Make a rough draft of your guest list

Choose your attendants--how many and whom

Start looking for your wedding dress

Pick your colors

Plan your theme or style

Pick your date

Pick your ceremony venue

Pick your reception venue

Pick who is going to marry you (minister, officiant, etc)

Reserve your date at your venue

Find a caterer

Find a cake

Find a photographer

Find a DJ or band

Get engagement photo (if you want)

Start a fitness routine (if you want)

6 to 12 Months out

Order wedding dress

Book vendors if you have not already

Have your food and cake tastings

Create your gift registry

Decide on your flowers

Research hotel rooms for out of town guests

Shop for attendant dresses

Shop for attendant accessories

Set up transportation

Finalize guest list for the wedding

Finalize the guest list for the rehearsal dinner

Get everyone's mailing addresses including spellings and names of their significant others.

Finalize beverage and catering details.

Make a list of all of your vendors include what you need to send them and when it is due.

3 to 6 Months out

Book the rehearsal dinner

Let all attendees of rehearsal and rehearsal dinner know the basic details

Reserve any rentals ie chairs, tables, tents, etc

Order or make wedding favors

Buy undergarments for your dress

Buy shoes

Get dress fitting

Order attendant outfits

Finalize invitations for wording

Order invitations or start to make them

Send any deposits out

Finalize ceremony readings

Do a makeup and hair trial.

Make child care arrangements if necessary

Finalize your appointments to have hair, makeup and nails done. Make sure you allow enough time to get to the ceremony on time.

Shop for wedding rings.

Finalize honeymoon plans.

Book honeymoon.

Make sure you have your passports

Mail save the date cards if you are using them

Finalize reception menu

6 to 8 Weeks out

Mail out invitations

Talk to vendors to make sure they have everything they need ie color samples, final decisions

Confirm wedding party have all ordered their outfits

Shop for or make thank you gifts for attendants

Write thank you cards for any early wedding presents including shower gifts

Final dress fitting--bring shoes and undergarments

3 to 4 Weeks out

Finalize booking for rehearsal dinner

Send out rehearsal dinner information

Apply for marriage license

Obtain marriage license

Finalize wedding vows, readings

Give photographer list of photos you need to have

Finalize song list for ceremony and reception

Set up a time line for the day including appointments for hair and when toasts will be done

Confirm wedding night or honeymoon accommodations

Pick up your wedding rings if you have not already

Find something old, something new, something borrowed, something blue

Purchase your guest book, candles etc

Track down anyone who has not RSVP

1 to 2 Weeks Out

Give your caterer and venue final head counts

Make a seating chart

Pick up your dress

Finalize arrival times and wedding time line with vendors

Come up with a contingency plan in case of bad weather

Get a facial or a massage and relax

Make a list of everything you need to bring with you the morning of the wedding

The Day Before

Make sure everything you need to get ready is packed including rings and marriage license

Get final payments together for vendors

Get tips ready

Make sure someone is setting up anything that needs to be done pre-ceremony or packing anything up after

Have a manicure and a pedicure

Have rehearsal dinner

Give attendants their gifts

The Big Day

Get plenty of sleep

Have your hair and makeup done

Get dressed

Get to the location

Marry the one you love

Ignore what ever went wrong

Have a wonderful time talking to family and friends

Dance

After the Honeymoon

Write and send thank you cards

Exchange any duplicate gifts

Have your wedding dress cleaned and preserved

About 4 to 8 weeks out, talk to your photographer about the wedding album

Choose photos for parents or siblings

Suggested Budget Categories

Major Categories

Church
Reception Site
Food and Beverages
Attire
Transportation
Honeymoon
Stationery
Photographer/Videographer
Attendant gifts
DJ
Decorations
Flowers
Miscellaneous Expenses

Category Breakdowns

Ceremony Site:
Church rental or ceremony site fee

Officiant fee
Transportation

Reception Site:
Food
Cake
Beverages including liquor
Decorations
Guest book
Tent rental
Chair and table rentals
Wait staff/bartenders
Tablecloths
Plates, cups, silverwares, napkins
Wedding Favors
DJ or Band
Centerpieces

Rehearsal Dinner:
Cost of officiant
Transportation
Gifts for attendants

Attire:
Tuxedo
Wedding dress

Alterations
Accessories
Undergarments
Shoes
Veil/head piece
Hair/Makeup
Manicure/Pedicure
Dress cleaning after ceremony

Photography:

Photographer
Videographer
Album
Parents Album
Extra Prints of Photos

Stationery:

Save the date cards
Invitations including response cards
Thank you cards
Ceremony programs
Stamps for envelopes
Calligraphy

Flowers:

Bouquets for bride and bridesmaids

Boutonnieres for groom, groomsmen and fathers
Corsages for mothers
Centerpieces for tables
Decorations for church
Flower girls basket

Honeymoon:
Plane tickets
Travel Agents
Passports
Cruise Line
Hotel
Transportation

Miscellaneous:
Guest book
Toasting flutes
Envelope Holder
Ring Bearer's Pillow
Marriage License
Gratuities
Envelope Basket/Holder

Wedding Day Wardrobe Checklist

Gown
Veil
Train (if separate)
Shoes
Panties
Bra/Corset
Garter
Something Old
Something Blue
Something Borrowed
Something New
Earrings
Necklace
Bracelet
Panty Hose/Stockings
Hairpiece

<u>Bridal Emergency Kit Suggestions</u>

Safety pins
Clear nail polish
Aspirin
Bobby pins
Nail file
Hand wipes/Moist towelettes
Hair spray
Small sewing kit
Mints
Facial Tissue
Lipstick
Extra Stockings
Some extra cash
Tampons

Suggested conversations

Where are you going to live after you are married?   His place, your place, some place new?

Where do you ultimately want to live? A house, apartment, condo? What part of the country or world? City or Suburb?

Do you want to travel? Long term or vacations?

Are you going to have kids? If so, are you planning to wait or have them right away?

Is one of you going to stay home with the kids? Will you use daycare?

Are you combining your money or keeping separate accounts?

Will you have a set budget? How will it be split up?

How are you going to split the chores?

Are you going to have pets? What kind?

How are you going to handle holidays with your respective families? Visit each every year? Alternating years?

Do you plan to exchange gifts for birthdays, Valentine's Day or is it not that important to you?

Are you going to raise your kids in a religion?

Have you told each other all of your dirt secrets?

Do you have an debt? If so, how will you deal with it?

What is your credit score?

Where do you want to be in 10 years? 20? 30?

What are your retirement goals or dreams?

What is your career goal? Will it require going back to school or relocating?

How will you handle your in-laws? What is the line that they can't cross?

Where do you stand on major political issues such as abortion, gun control etc?

What is the worst thing that ever happened to you?

What was your childhood like?

How would you do it differently if you have kids?

What level of privacy do you expect? For example, is it OK to open each other's mail?

Do you have any physical problems or illness?

More from EJ Divitt:

Etiquette As I Learned It

http://amzn.com/B00E6XCPHS

Have you ever found yourself at a loss as to what to say to someone at a funeral? Been overwhelmed at the thought of writing a thank you card? You have good intentions but just need a little help? This book is for you.

This is a guide to etiquette in every day situations and special occasions including weddings, funerals and thank you cards. It includes an all new etiquette quiz with answers at the back of the book.

Coming early 2014

Things Every Goddess Should Know

If life is a game, this is the guide book. Filled with advice for women on relationships, self improvement, love, money, health and much more.

EJ's Blogs:

The Etiquette blog

http://etiquetteasilearned it.blogspot.com/

The Things Every Goddess
Should Know blog

http://thingseverygoddess .blogspot.com/